SUNSHINE

Additional copies of this book are available
by mail:
Send $10.00 plus $3.00 shipping and
handling per book to Curtis Jones
926 Spring Rd., N.W., Washington, D.C.
20010
or

Telephone number 1-202-286-2728
E-Mail Sunset1052@yahoo.com
Website sunrisetosunsetpoetry.com
Facebook: Curtis Jones
Amazonbooks.com

Cover Photography:

Printed in the United States of America by
Morris Publishing®
3212 East Highway 30
Kearney, NE 68847
1-800-650-7888

Acknowledgments

A special thank you to Kelsey L. Swanson
for proof-reading my book,
To Cheryle Adams for her encouragement
and technical support,
To ShaRon Meshack for the spirit of her
technical expertise.

And a very special thank you to Ivy Jones
and Ben Johnson for the final reading.

Also, A special thank you to the
Arena Stage at the Mead Center
For American Theater
In Washington, DC. for much inspiration.

Dedications

This book is dedicated to my parents:
Mr. and Mrs. Arlee Jones, my two
daughters, Wanda and Shani, my
spiritual daughter, ShaRon Meshack,
my brother Harold, and sisters Arlene
and Janet, and to all of my family members
and friends.

And a special dedication to my loving sister,
LaVoyne, and to my loving brother,
Richard.

Table Of Contents

The Cosmos

The forever changing universe…
A quest for the ultimate truth.
A revelation in cosmology…
On a timescale that defies imagination.

And as questions arise….
And theories abound,
Much is still unknown…
About where it all came from.

For some will say, God created everything.
And others will say, evolution was in the mix,
With a cosmic calendar traveling at the speed of light...
Filled with a cosmic soup of the elements of life.

And from a Divine spirit, to the Big Bang theory…
The sense of wonder is familiar, not distant.
Because it lives in our hearts of the notion…
To thrive on the ideas of exploration.

For we'll venture through stargates and constellations….
After the matter of explosions from super novae.
And we'll look beyond the event horizon of a black hole…
To see a time warp in the fabric of space and time.

And as gravity holds court over the stars and planets…
We'll fasten our seatbelts, in light of the ghost.
To blastoff from planet Earth in search of life…
Discovering new galaxies, in the vastness of the cosmos.

When The Sun Shines

There is no mistaking the beauty…
When the sun is up and shining.
And there is no underestimating the life….
That it gives to a thriving world.

For the benefits come to all the earth…
As we prepare the victory garden,
With golden rays from our precious sun…
Delivering on the goods we'll reap from the harvest.

And the reward is for all to see…
This planet teeming with life,
With more in store for us today…
As we'll stand by to receive more tomorrow.

Because the sun will come out…
To take its place in the cosmos.
And we'll be grateful every time….
As time goes by, when the sun shines.

Intelligent Design

The universe, is as mysterious as it seems…
Enough for us to wonder about its origin.
And there're plenty of theories going around…
With many speculations that abound.

Because we all have our notions about life…
But only one is of faith,
And that's in the belief of a Creator…
For out of love, we were made to feel His spirit.

And throughout the cosmos, and on planet Earth…
The designs of intelligence are evident.
Because we see it in the relativity of things…
From the stars in space, down to the human race.

And from the largest, to the smallest of things…
A designer is the subject of the matter,
Of how all these things came about…
Without seeing God's face, to even doubt it.

Mankind

The story about us…
More than what we know.
The mysterious history…
Fueling the speculation.

Because we have the creation story…
Coming down through time.
And we have the story of evolution…
Running along its timeline.

And in our footsteps…
We find wars and peace and reconstruction.
And in the tracks of our tears…
We've left behind a tale of death and destruction.

And as we've had our ups and downs…
We've managed to make some progress.
And with our technology on the run…
We're racing to buy some time in the process.

For our future is in the event…
Of shooting for the stars.
And we'll drag along all of the baggage
That we'll manage, to warrant an advantage.

Because we've been on the move…
From hunter-gatherer to city dweller.
And we'll settle for nothing less in mind…
Than what's coming, for the survival of mankind.

Enjoy This Life

You only go around once in this world…
No second chance to get it right.
One life of happiness to pursue…
To stop and smell the flowers given to you.

And drink the coffee…
Sip the fine wine,
Be of good character…
And be wise with your time.

To kick up your heels…
Click the red shoes three times.
For home is where peacefulness resides…
Where family and friendships cross property lines.

So, with love, enjoy this life…
While laughing in the face of adversity,
And smiling with your eyes on the prize…
To just be happy and grateful to be alive.

Children Of The Stars

Of everything God created in the universe...
We're made from the same elements,
As from the stardust that falls to the earth...
To be a part of us all from birth.

For from the ground we became...
As stars from the heavenly realm.
With the moon and the sun raising a family...
Providing sustenance of treasure throughout the ages.

And as we grow with insight...
It's within each starchild to shine.
For the brightness to live on...
As we go through the phases of time.

For we're the children of the stars...
From the makeup of the celestial cosmos.
And from the spirit that's within it...
We're homegrown from the soul of this planet.

God Bless The Child

God blesses the child…
Who realizes their needs,
To receive more than enough…
When they work hard for the proceeds.

Because there are certain things in life…
That need to be addressed.
For a person to go through…
In order to be blessed.

For blessings will come to the child…
Who knows how to get their own,
For when they leave home…
For when they are grown.

Because guidance and direction…
Will lead them to righteousness.
Where an everlasting power…
Will supply everything for enlightenment.

And God bless the child…
For not just standing around.
And for all the good that's been done…
The blessings will abound.

God's Children

We are all God's children...
And this is His planet.
And He created life on earth.
For it to be the home we'll inherit.

And for it to be filled...
With plenty of righteousness.
With provisions to share in our care...
For the daily needs of our happiness.

And above all of that...
Are His future plans for us,
For the time we'll spend in eternity...
To be cherished between Heaven and paradise.

Because it's all up to the Father...
In relating to His children,
In what He expects of them as a family...
And in what they'll respect about Him.

Born To Love...

We're not born with hatred...
It's learned as we grow.
Because as a child, our instincts show...
We were born to love.

For as children, we play...
To be color blind.
With a time of innocence...
For enjoying unconditional friendships.

But as we grow older...
We'll be a witness to the truth,
About a world that's waiting...
With the experience of a rude awakening.

And the reality of it all...
Now after we're grown,
Is that we were born to love...
And we'll reap what we sow.

The Sweet Smell Of Success

It's aromatic of the nature...
With a fragrance of prosperity,
Distinguishing it from the rest...
It's the sweet smell of success.

And it comes when we look within...
To examine what we're after.
For the ingredients to blend in...
With the essence we'll manufacture.

Because it has a unique scent...
Compared to money well spent.
And if it don't make dollars...
It don't make sense...

But sometimes success goes beyond...
The boundary lines of wealth and fame.
To just smell the flowers of love that grow...
From the ground floor, right in our very homes.

Never Underestimate A Woman

For too long, women have been underestimated...
And devalued of what they're really worth.
But pound-for-pound it's been understood...
That from their past record, they have nothing to prove.

Because it's been a misunderstanding...
Of the things of strength that are demanding,
But of the ones that have been for men to do...
It's for a female, to measure up with endurance.

And the difference is made up...
In her willingness to communicate.
Because she has all the needs and skills of education...
Along with all of the assets for procreation.

For a woman has all of the abilities...
To achieve just as much as a man.
But of course, all that she'll need from him...
Is his life-giving seed, with his love to give.

Then There Was You

She lights up a room with her beauty…
To brighten up any day.
And she charms the hearts of hearts…
Then there was you.

She wears the finest clothes…
With a priceless personality to match.
And she's regal in her sophistication…
Then there was you.

She says the right words…
With smiles and laughter at the right time.
Because she's educated and congenial…
Then there was you.

And she's loved by everyone…
Just like everyone loves you.
And if there was her…
Then there had to be you.

Beauty Of The Century

The loving thought of a creation…
Had you in mind to represent,
That one of a kind…
A woman, that was Heaven sent.

And from this century into the next…
Beautiful women would have come and gone.
But the essence of your beauty will live on…
To be compared to none.

Because you're a woman of distinction
With inner qualities separating you from the rest.
And it's regal with an aura that surrounds you…
That's what makes you the best.

For you have the stature of a living queen…
With loveliness in the eyes that are beholding,
From which we'll hold in the palms of our hands…
To be held right next to our hearts

Because your face radiates with love…
It's more precious than can be imagined,
With the stature of a cosmopolitan look…
That could grace the cover of any book…

And from the inside out…
And from the past and present, we'll see,
That you hold the title to be called…
The beauty of the century.

You've Got The Look

There's something about the look…
That stops people in their tracks.
For some people just have it …
And some people don't.

But you were born with it…
And you still possess it,
A look that can't be explained…
It's a look that can't be described.

Because you don't have to be the prettiest…
You don't have to have the finest figure,
You don't have to have the best hairdo…
But you do have to have something special.

And whatever it is about you…
It's factored into the "It" book.
And from all that we know about you…
Is that you've got the look.

Keep Her Laughing

As long as she likes your jokes…
You're making good ground.
And if she still loves your sense of humor…
It'll cancel your trip to the dog pound.

Because she'll want to keep you around.
For the medicine you prescribe,
In helping her condition…
With happiness, to keep her attention.

Because while she's laughing…
She'll forget about what you've done,
Long enough not to remember…
Some of the things you didn't do.

So keep her smiling…
It makes good sense.
And keep her laughing…
On the account of your expense.

A Woman Scorned

There's nothing worse...
Than a woman who's been scorned.
For she has her pride...
And when that's shattered, Lord have mercy on your soul.

Because all she'll think about...
Is how good she was to you.
And after the memory has played itself out...
All hell will break loose.

For when a woman is jilted...
Don't even try to figure out her mind.
And forget about negotiating and explaining...
For you'll just be wasting your time.

Because she doesn't want to hear it...
She's seen and heard enough already.
And if you cross her path now...
You'll be real sorry for it.

For she only knows...
The contempt of being shamed and scorned,
And you're to blame for the disdain...
And you'll wish that you were never born.

In The Doghouse

A direct result of being bad…
Is the punishment that comes.
And for a man, if he's a louse…
He'll end up in the doghouse.

A place where bad guys go…
To be with their best friend,
Being accused of acting like them…
When things go wrong for him.

And he'll accept his predicament…
To take it like a man.
Then, to come through with a precious gift and a kiss…
Hoping to end the rift with a master plan.

Because he knows he won't be there long…
Especially if he plays his cards right.
And if all goes well throughout the days ahead…
He'll be out of the doghouse, and back in the bedroom tonight.

"The Good Guy"

The good guy usually doesn't have enough money…
Because he's always giving it away.
For somebody is always asking for more…
And he just can't say no.

The good guy is usually a good listener…
And always used as a sounding board.
For when people come with their drama…
He never turns them away at the door.

The good guy is usually taken for granted…
Because with him, they usually have the advantage.
For they know how far they can go…
Before he'll do anything to stop it.

And the good guy will probably finish last…
Because he puts everyone before himself.
But he knows he'll be rewarded…
By coming in first on the welcome list.

"Dancing To Her Tune"

When she says jump…
He says, "How high."
Racing to spring into action…
At the whim of her discretion.

And when she tells him to go…
He says, "To where and how far."
To the ends of the earth for sure…
Going all the way for her.

Because he knows what's good for him…
Enough to either sink or swim.
And not to make any waves…
But to do just what she says.

Because she has a list of things for him…
And it's called, honey-do.
And he'd better complete it…
To avoid what he'll have to go through.

For he'll have to do the dance…
With the music that's made for her delight.
Dancing to her tune…
For all the reasons why.

The Power Of Music

Enchanted by the empowerment of its notes...
Engaged in the magic of it.
Endorphins dancing in our minds...
As the sound of music transcends time.

For it's more than just hearing it...
Because it's full of a meaningful bliss.
And it means more than just listening to it...
Because it's full of the feelings we can't forget.

And as we dream upon our dreams...
The music will take us there,
Everywhere we envision its unlimited power...
Places on a mission, on the hour.

And with the force of its rhythm on course...
We'll follow the melody of Orpheus.
And as the inflection of lyrics descend into our souls...
We'll let our emotions flow with the composition.

To be carried away with the orchestration...
In love with every beat that touches our hearts.
Never to underestimate the mystique...
That resides in the power of music.

The Super Information Highway

The information infrastructure…
The dynamics of the spider's web,
Racing through cyberspace…
To invade our personal world.

Because the technological wizardry online…
Feeds a computer savvy international pirate,
Sharing his wares, as fast as the speed of light…
With the black widow of the worldwide web.

And accessing our files, is "Big Brother," of the net.
And hacking away, is the super highway bandit.
While both, steal, blackmail and email our identity…
With power from the electronic fiber-optic light.

And with the downloading quickness of a lightning flash…
A virus can shake the foundation of every website,
Going to the very core of every hard drive…
With a shockwave of poison making the connection.

For in the vast networking of a wireless ocean…
We'll surf in the virtual reality of a geometric storm.
All to be caught up in the magic on the internet…
By the digital geomagnetic force, of the Super Information
Highway.

The Lie

They're living a lie...
And lying to live,
Even when they're lying...
They think they're telling the truth.

For they'll lie just because...
It becomes a habit to like it.
Even when we don't buy it...
They're still trying to sell it.

Because they're always lying in wait...
And waiting to lie,
To catch us holding the scales...
To put a blindfold over our eyes.

But their lies have been told too often...
With so many holes, they won't hold water.
Especially when they're coming on strong...
We know they've got nothing going on.

For in the end...
Their lies will tell on them.
Because with the truth to behold...
Their nose will grow, like Pinocchio's.

"Uncle Sam"

He was there at the foundation of our nation…
When taxation without representation was the cry.
But as soon as we gained our independence…
Our freedom was a dollar sign in his eye.

And from counterfeit speeches…
He seldom offered a break.
And just for the sake of it…
He was always on the take.

With his foolish federal spending…
And guaranteed government waste,
Leaving a tale of prohibition…
With "Uncle Sam" getting more than a taste.

And through many recessions and the Great Depression…
Americans still stood tall.
Working their way back to the top…
While Sam controlled the capital.

And, oh yes, he was there when needed…
Pumping billions into a premeditated war.
Sending our proud troops marching on…
While the bill was being paid by the poor.

And, yes, he's been our uncle…
Our country 'tis of thee.
And now we know what his name really means…
Because "Uncle Sam" wants you… to Send-All-Money.

The Eleventh Hour

Time is always running out...
And we're always on the edge of discovering,
That in a vast universe of time...
It's always the eleventh hour

Because we live in the moment...
Forgetting about the past too fast.
And when we pause to reference it...
It's already, the eleventh hour.

For we know the speed of light ...
Travels faster than the eye can track it.
So we'll try to catch a falling star...
In, the eleventh hour.

Because we can feel the urgency...
Of how fast time flies,
And the pressing issues that circle the globe...
To stop on a dime, in the eleventh hour.

And we'll "wait on" what we've got coming...
For a lifelong job, well done.
And we'll hope it's enough to cash in on...
In the eleventh hour.

"Don't Disgrace The Uniform!"

There are certain uniforms…
That are put on for the effect.
And when they're worn proudly …
They'll get the respect.

Because whoever wears it…
Knows why they signed up.
And whoever respects it…
Will do their best to measure up to it.

And that would be by the way…
In how they represent themselves.
And it would be in the order with things…
Of conducting their professional business.

And no matter if it's on or off the field…
Being a civilian or in military service.
Remember why it's worn…
And "Don't disgrace the uniform!"

Battlefield Warriors

Brave soldiers at home on the Western Front...
Coming off the front lines of war in the east.
Soldiers coming back with injuries of all kinds...
Some physical, and some invisible to our eyes.

Because we can see the disability of the ones...
Enough to feel their pain and distress.
But what we don't see on the faces...
Is the Post Traumatic Stress that needs to be addressed.

For the cause and affects of doing battle...
Have been known to rattle the nerves of the strongest.
And after the fact, it doesn't matter how it happened
Whether in the line of fire or by accident.

And it's not that they want sympathy...
For doing the job they signed up to fight for.
Because what stands behind the pride of the uniform...
Is the courage of a soldier, with everything to live for.

And out of respect, while they're in transition...
We should be standing at attention, shoulder-to-shoulder,
At the ready, to do all that we can and more...
To fight for the quality of life, for our Battlefield Warriors.

Baptism By Fire

Soldiers on the front lines…
Under the gun, stressed out about thoughts of war.
Soldiers under fire, minding the business…
Doing battle with the enemy of their conscience.

Because it's kill or be killed…
Virgins of the war with reality.
Dealing with ultimate warfare for the first time…
A professional in self-preservation in the meantime.

Running scared, trying to be brave…
Bombs bursting everywhere.
Standing tall, having the courage…
With convictions of having the right to be there.

And as hell comes to the theatre…
Heaven awaits to claim the victory.
And from the last gunshot, to the smoke in their eyes…
The prayers are for peace, after the baptism by fire.

Wounded Warriors

Coming home from being battle-tested…
A homecoming for our valiant soldiers,
Coming home from a war…
That was waged to be won by sacrifice.

And from the front lines to the combat zone…
A purple heart was given for courage.
And a promise was made to all veterans…
To share in the aftercare of their service.

For the rehabilitation begins…
At the moment of their injuries.
Because we owe it to them…
To be there in the aid of their recovery.

Because they're among the proud and the brave…
Not asking for much in the way,
But just to be respected as an American soldier…
Who volunteered to put on the uniform.

And it goes beyond the trauma…
Not to be forgotten about after the drama.
And it all comes with a compassion to do more…
To all we can do now, for our wounded warriors.

World War Two

When World War One was over
It was to put an end to all wars.
But along came another one…
Calling on all soldiers from their nations to march on.

And some were volunteers…
For the battles that had to be fought.
And others were conscripted…
For the fight of their lives, that had to be won.

Because this was an unforgiving war…
Of unprecedented proportions.
It was a world war again…
Between the Axes powers and the Allied forces.

And it was by no means…
Anything less than what it meant.
And it had to be stopped…
More or less, at all cost.

Because it was to change the face of the world…
For all who would, to take up arms for the cause.
Because it was WORLD WAR TWO…
And there was no time or place to pause.

For they had to fight fire with fire…
From the air, land and sea.
And by the time the smoke cleared…
Standing with peace and freedom, was the victory.

"The Drill"

It's routine,
To wake up to a day…
With work and obligations to fulfill,
You know the drill.

And it's standard procedure…
On a regular course of action,
To go through the motions…
On a daily basis.

And often repeated in life…
Are the mistakes not heeded.
And over and over again…
There you go again.

And just like the soldiers…
Training to march off to war,
Knowing when, and when not to kill…
They know the drill.

An Education

We may play around with it…
From kindergarten to college,
Balancing the act of an education…
With some serious side effects on knowledge.

And we can't let neglectfulness…
Dominate the view of intelligence.
Because the charts and the test…
Will only tell of the average.

For the homework will show…
If learning came first.
Leading to a better future…
Getting more than what's on the surface.

Because it can be fun to learn the process…
With hard work as a means to an end to take
And through public, private, charter or home schooling…
Teachers must trust in themselves to educate.

For there's a system in place…
Of academics, money and power.
Promoting self-interest for many reasons…
That go beyond our imagination to fathom.

Somebody Loves You

Somewhere, there's somebody who cares about you…
You can count on that.
Because out of billions on this planet…
There's got to be someone who loves you.

But the odds are against it…
And nine times out of ten you'll loose,
While the degree of love you expect…
Will be by the decision you choose.

And to be chosen…
Will let you know you're wanted.
But the motive of their advance…
Will have to hold up under a microscope.

And to choose with judgment…
While the jury is still out,
Means taking a chance…
Before the verdict comes in.

And as you try to make sure of the source…
You'll know when love comes upon you.
Because when you search you'll find…
That the chemistry of true love, will find you.

You're Special

You're special...
As special as they come.
And the reasons are of many to impart...
Becoming of the goodness from your heart.

For the record shows...
And the list of accomplishments is long,
Filled with the wonderful things you've done...
Since the day you were born.

And from the past onto the present...
You've been absolutely remarkable,
And a beautiful person in the event...
That has earned the Red Carpet treatment.

Because you're special in the makeup...
To be of the essence,
Always with the difference...
Of the good in you to reference.

The Thinking Path

There's a road we go down…
Where your deep thoughts go with you.
And they'll follow you on the path…
Of conscious enlightenment.

Where you're placed in a state of nirvana…
With intelligence relative to the surroundings.
And time is of the essence…
Where your feelings are of the highest priority.

For you'll study with the ancients…
Resigned to a long and storied tradition,
Of burning the midnight oil…
With success achieved after much failure.

And you'll reach the city of great dreamers…
Who take their imaginations to the limit.
Having grandiose visions…
Where truth carries more weight than science fiction.

And you'll walk through doors of understanding…
Taking steps from expressions of life with reverence,
Where there's always a different point of view…
On the thinking path, of many things to pursue.

When The Sun Rises

At first light, the day begins…
As it never fails on its journey,
To start its climb at the dawning…
Spreading its warmth across the waters of life.

And upon the shores await the morning dew…
Collected with the mist of the rushing waves,
That splash upon the wind-swept faces…
Filtering in with the rays of sunlight.

For the beginning of a precious day continues…
Strolling over meadows and rolling hills,
While the sun is still rising to shine…
Up mountainsides, and down into the valleys.

And the rest of the world in slumber…
Will have to wait their turn on the rock,
To look over the horizon…
Anticipating the time, when the sun rises.

Live Up To Your Potential

Each one of us has to learn in life…
How to turn on their eternal light.
To find their way through a maze of darkness…
That defines their run on the road to progress.

Because inside of you is furnished…
With gifts in every room of your essence,
Waiting to be examined with interest…
By the hands of your perseverance.

And to reach into the very depths…
Of your inner and outer strengths,
Realizing all the reasons to get busy…
To live up to your potential.

Because you have everything to live for…
With nothing to remove any doubt,
Of your ability to rise up…
To place your flag on the highest mountain.

And when you're standing on top of the world…
Look up into the sky,
For now, you're reaching for the stars…
Because now, they're in your eyes.

This Day Belongs To You

When you awaken today...
Look outside the window,
To imagine what's over the horizon for you...
As blessings await beyond the view.

And as it may, be glad...
That you're able to get up out of the bed.
Because life is fresh in the airways of time...
From the dawning of a beautiful sunrise.

Because it offers you another chance...
To dance with the daylight,
And to be with the ones you love...
To enjoy the life-giving sunshine from above.

And it's for you to be happy...
To explore what's in Heaven and on earth to get.
Because this day belongs to you...
To relish, before the sun sets.

Leave No Stone Unturned

Don't be first to throw the rock…
Especially if it's at your own house.
But instead, let justice be found…
Before burying the hatchet.

And look into the allegations…
Checking on all the motivations,
In the best-case scenario…
Without prejudice intentions.

And you'll see the jagged cliffs looming above…
While the polished stones rest below,
Waiting to be overturned in time…
By the truth in the wind, rushing in with the tides.

And the evidence uncovered…
Is after a trial inspection has learned,
That to be sure, is to see for yourself…
By leaving no stone unturned.

Nothing Good Comes Easy

When it's too easy for some things…
They don't last for long,
To be as good as most things…
When they've earned the right to belong.

Because when it's taken for granted…
There's no accepting the value.
Becoming to nothing…
Not respected for anything.

And as easy comes, easy goes…
To be without a care when it disappears.
Because the good of it doesn't last long enough…
To get past the bad effort that reappears.

For nothing good comes easy…
And it never becomes treasured,
Especially when it's too easy to let it go and forget…
Not realizing, just how much you need to keep it.

Live, While Living

It's one thing to be alive…
With all the reasons in the world, to live and let live.
But it's something else to live a life…
While living it to the fullest.

Because to live while living…
Is in the quality you'll give it.
And to love every minute of it…
Is what you'll be giving it.

While venturing out to explore…
Searching for new tomorrows and more.
Learning all what's good to know…
From the experiences in life as you grow.

And it's essential, to not ever lose sight…
Of the happiness you can have,
By living it up, while you're living…
Enjoying it all, while you can.

Character, Matters

A character walked into the place...
Everyone looked.
It put on an act...
And everyone wondered.

Who can it be?
Does it matter to suppose.
Who cares to know?
When it comes and goes.

But it does make a difference in judgment...
And a matter of fact, it always will.
For characterization leaves the impression...
That's left behind in the courts of public opinion.

And we'll add to it, waiting to subtract...
Giving it the benefit of doubt.
Hopefully in the expression, for it to win out...
Because character matters, on all accounts.

True To Your Word

On the account of being trusted and respected...
Let your words instill the value.
For in the face of social regard...
Hard is the truth, to live up to.

Especially when your fidelity is challenged...
And your integrity comes under fire,
While forthcoming is the light of day...
Withstanding the areas of gray.

For the truth will shine with the sun...
As each golden ray pierces the page,
Where nothing is written down...
But for your words, to hold its ground.

And true to your word...
Goes beyond a handshake that complies,
With a guarantee to back it up with results...
From in your heart, where the truth abides.

The Grace Of God

By the grace of God...
We've managed this far,
To come to an understanding...
Of the power of His love.

Because we know it's by His grace...
That we're still standing.
And we know it's with compassion...
That we'll be remembered in Heaven.

For we'll be kept in His mind...
To maintain a righteous life on earth.
And we'll remain in His memory...
From imperfection to Paradise.

And wherever we may be found...
In whatever may be the place.
We'll know our survival is with mercy...
And by the will of God's grace.

Jehovah

Jehovah is His personal name…
It's found in the Webster's dictionary and the Bible.
And along with all of His titles…
It's synonymous with His power.

For He is the God of all things…
And the Father of all creation.
He's the Ancient of Days…
And the Almighty Power.

And He's the Alpha and the Omega…
The beginning and the end,
The past, the present and the future…
The first and the last.

And as His name has been known for ages…
It's been minimized next to His persona.
But He did say, "That on that Great Day…
They will all, know my name."

Because now it's being used even more…
Just as it was from the days of old.
And it's called upon in many a language…
By the name He gave us to know, Jehovah.

Jesus

Many on this earth...
Know the name of Jesus,
And for what He represented...
Since the day of His birth.

For He was baptized in the Jordan River...
To be the Promised One.
And He walked this earth as the Messiah...
To spread faith, hope and love around.

And through the message in His ministry...
He addressed the needs of mankind.
And during His lifetime, He made preparations...
For our redemption, through a resurrection.

Because His name means, our salvation...
As He became a ransom sacrifice for the cause.
For He is the Word, that saves us...
The Anointed One, Christ Jesus.

The Holy Spirit

God's invisible force…
Has been there since Paradise lost.
And it was poured out in the Upper Room…
On the day of Pentecost.

And filled with the Holy Spirit…
Were the Chosen Ones,
When it sat upon their heads…
With tongues of fire.

And to the rest of the world…
The Holy Spirit went out,
With the powers that be…
In helping people believe.

For God loved the world so much…
He sent his Holy Active Force to us,
To be a helpmate for all…
And for the sake of us all.

The Covenant

He gave His word to Adam and Eve…
To be obedient, and they would live forever.
And through them, would come a family…
To live in peace on earth for eternity.

He set a rainbow in the sky…
As a promise to Noah.
Never to destroy life in the world again…
By waters from the deep, and from the heavens.

And He made a covenant with Abraham…
Promising through Him, a great nation,
And of a King Priest that would come…
To lead mankind back to perfection.

For God sacrificed His only-begotten son…
As a covenant for our redemption.
And it was by His shed blood…
That we'll receive our salvation.

Life And Death

These are the basics…
The bottom line.
We're born to live a number of years…
Then along the way, we die.

It's cut and dry…
The beginning and the ending.
It's all a part of living…
That is, the standard.

For we don't know our last call…
The day and hour is not known.
So in the meantime, we don't worry…
We just kick up our heels and go on.

Because if we try to dwell on it…
We'll lose our reasons for living.
And end up losing out on happiness…
To be preoccupied with our fate in things.

And when the end comes…
We'll just accept it to be.
And lay down all of our hopes and faith…
To be raised up, in God's memory.

The Resurrections

In the Garden of Eden...
The promise of a seed was foretold.
And it was to redeem mankind from sin...
To be saved by a death caused by Satan.

For now, there was a need for a resurrection...
Because the first human pair had disobeyed God.
And a volunteer was sent from the Heavenly realm...
To be the ransom sacrifice for the cause.

And after the death of the only begotten son of prophecy...
God performed the miracle of a resurrection.
And He became the resurrection, the truth and the life...
In the name, of Jesus Christ.

Because He gave up His precious life...
To ensure that we had a chance to live forever.
And after His resurrection and ascension into Heaven...
It became a reality, for us to receive the blessings.

And it will be on His return to Earth...
A first resurrection of the First Fruits.
And then it will be, for a Heavenly calling...
To be of kings and priests, when God's kingdom comes.

And then, there was a second resurrection...
Of the righteous and the unrighteous.
And all were to stand before the throne...
On Judgment Day, for the inheritance of an earthly home.

For it must come to pass
For all these things to happen.
Because in Paradise, there will be no more need...
For any more, resurrections.

Spirituality

Deep-rooted in faith…
A tree grows to great heights.
Spreading its branches of hope…
To the leaves of enlightenment to behold.

And it will bear the fruit…
From the seeds that were Heaven-sent.
And for the sowing of righteousness…
To flourish with the reaping of nourishment.

For the grapes of the vine without malice…
Will pour as pure wine from the chalice.
With the partaking of the Word…
In prayer with the Spirit of the Lord.

And in each religion, it's without separation…
As it reaches across the aisle, to all denominations.
With an understanding of the ghost in the reality…
That relates to the love, from the host of spirituality.

Religions

Religions of the world...
From the major to the minor,
From the fanatical to the idealistic...
From the spiritualistic to the mystic.

And oh, how their gardens grow...
From all of the seeds that have been planted.
And the battles that have been fought...
Just look, at what we've got!

And all in the name of religion...
Many have fallen while believing,
That their God was to be the one...
To help win the war, for the true believers.

For all the roads seem to lead there...
Somewhere between Heaven and Earth
Then, to be touched by God's Holy Spirit...
For all of the good people in religions, to inherit.

Hope

Have hope in the things…
You want to come true.
And believe in yourself…
Enough, to follow through.

And keep hope alive, for the life of you…
For as long as you can,
To forever and a day…
Make it happen your way.

For on a good day…
It's your best day,
Every day to be better…
Hoping for more, to be better than ever.

Because being hopeful builds confidence…
In the belief of what you can achieve.
All within the faith of what you'll receive…
To be enough, for you to be pleased.

A Matter Of Faith

It's a matter of faith…
That our day will be blessed after the sunrise.
It's a matter of faith…
That we'll live through the night after sunset.

And it's a matter of faith…
To trust in the words of the Lord.
And it's a matter in the reality…
If we'll be worthy of a reward.

For in faith, we'll believe…
In the power of the Holy Spirit,
And of what it can do for us…
With its love, that comes to us.

And it's a matter of faith…
To have hope for tomorrow,
And that we'll see another day…
God be willing, with many more days to follow.

A Divine Order

By the will of God...
It will be done.
For you to reap...
What you sow.

And by divine order...
It will materialize,
To be what you've planted...
To grow into what you deserve.

Because when your deeds are measured...
They'll weigh heavy on your heart,
To put your mind at ease...
When you're doing the right things.

And your soul will know...
When good things come around.
And it will be by a Divine Order...
For the fruits of your labor to abound.

Love Yourself

First, you have to love yourself...
Then, you can pass it on,
Giving it to others to receive...
A love in return that you'll need.

For self-love is a requirement...
It connects you with the environment,
While your mortal soul depends on it...
With your spirit making sure of it.

Because it starts with you...
Believing in yourself.
And it continues inside of you...
By loving what you do.

And when you decide it's alright...
To love yourself for a change.
You'll make room for some of the others...
To receive more of the same.

The Greatest Story Ever Told

A great story has been told in many languages…
With different variations in translations.
But the meaning is still the same…
Even when mankind's ideas about things have changed.

For we'll have different versions…
Of interpretations from theocratic scholars.
But the truth is in the text of a faith…
That shines with God's spirit in our hearts.

And as it was from the beginning of our creation…
It's been viewed as a revelation,
With theories of evolution abounding…
Challenging the Bible and its foundation.

But with the realization of an inspired story…
Being time-tested with words of love and truth,
It becomes of us through our souls, never to get old …
Because it's the Greatest Story ever told.

Evil Walks This Planet

There's more bad news in the world today...
Than we would ever like to hear about.
And as usual, it's unbalanced...
With the sin on earth, outweighing any doubt.

Because trouble never takes a holiday...
Even more so, in the safety of our homes.
For God gracefully comes in the front door...
While Satan slithers in from the rear.

And it will test anyone's imagination...
To think that things will get better.
And it would almost be criminal...
To believe in the increase of public safety.

Because the verdict is in...
There is evil amongst us.
And it's without mercy...
For the meek and the innocent.

And from all over the globe...
It's the same terror that stalks this earth...
And it's for the righteous ones to stand against it...
Because evil walks this planet.

Satan's Harvest

Seeds prepared for life's encounters...
The sowing,
The growing,
The reaping.

Seedlings in the springtime...
The saplings growing into majestic trees,
Of what life has brought to these...
Through the falling of the leaves.

And beware! The Grim Reaper is raking...
Not mistaking his crop,
Of all the followers for the taking...
Where sinning never stops.

And as the fruit becomes ripe for the picking...
It's separated from the rest.
And compared with the statistics...
It's a large crowd, for "Satan's Harvest!"

"Life, Is Like That!"

Life has twists and turns…
And the end comes upon us fast,
With one ticket to ride…
On the roller coaster of a lifetime.

Life has mountains to climb…
With valleys and rivers to traverse,
And of all the oceans to cross over…
From one-way to another.

Life is a decision-making process…
For the survivors to solve the equation.
But, like the lightning flashing…
The rush of time is passing.

For life has lessons for learning…
And it's full of many adventurous acts,
Written on the pages of living…
Foregoing, forgiving, foregone…for "Life is like that!"

At The End Of The Day

From off the lips of man, to the ears of God...
We'll hear the stories of days gone by.
And foretold are the reasons why to ask for mercy...
At the end of the day.

For on the dawning of a life...
With a lifetime to find the way,
Not lost in the night is the light...
At the end of the day.

And through it all...
Will come a time to pray,
With answers that await our progress...
At the end of the day.

And it's for our discernible works of character...
To leave a legacy on the steps of righteousness,
All on the grounds of the faith that doesn't fade...
From the love, from above, at the end of the day.

Temptation

It's hard to resist…
Some of those favorite things.
The ones that beckon for trouble to come…
With an invitation to follow along.

Because temptation walks…
Especially to stalk its prey,
Tuned into the frequency…
To catch you falling for its ways.

And the choice is there to make…
With the consequences to pay.
For if you dare to go there…
Beware of what awaits beyond the gates.

Because you'll feel, that it hurts so good…
To know, that you've got it bad.
For you can want…
What you know you shouldn't have.

For with temptation all around…
All of the time,
Your only offence is a good defense…
Because temptation, is the hardest thing to resist.

Changed Forever

There are moments in our lives…
That remain with us forever.
Leaving a mark that's not forgotten…
Changing us forever.

Like the tragedy on nine-one-one…
It changed a nation.
And now the world is changed as so…
Because psychologically, it was felt across the globe.

And anyone who understands America…
Recognizes our will to prevail.
And the changes we now have to make…
Are costing us dearly as well.

Because now we have more problems…
Emotionally affecting our well-being.
For this aggression was a force-multiplier…
Making believers of us all, to react to the challengers.

And if we didn't know then…
Now, we know better of the terror.
For we've seen and experienced enough already…
To know our state of freedom, has been changed forever.

Fatherhood

It comes at a time in life…
When a man sows his seed,
And he's expecting a plant, bearing fruit…
To grow from out of the garden.

And as he'll experience the symptoms…
Some of which we expect from a mother,
Eventually to be realized and related…
With the bonding of father and child.

Because he'll feel what she feels…
Of the spiritual nature of conception,
And how it passes on from childbearing…
To surpass the psychology of childrearing.

For it can only be explained…
Through the nature of fatherhood,
And in all the preparations from him…
With the great expectations, of the love he should give.

Father And Son

From a father to his son…
The gift of life is given.
And from wisdom in the words of being good…
He was to use through a life of manhood.

For he'll share in the knowledge…
Of a father's teachings about living,
For him to listen and learn…
About the things he'll need to discern.

Because one day, he'll have to measure up…
To the challenge from a world of decisions to make.
And then, to use his maturity to relate…
To make his own personal statement.

For a father's love…
Will come on strong with instructions.
For a son to realize…
His strength was for a reason.

Because their differences…
Will come together with understanding.
For a father to eventually know…
That his son, now stands on his own.

Father's Day

It's been much in the way…
Of just another day for him.
But finally it's being realized…
Of his importance in the family to be recognized.

And as he'll hope to be remembered…
He'll wait without anticipation.
Because the day used to just pass by…
Without much fanfare or celebration.

But as it's gradually being advertised…
His day is finally getting some respect.
Especially if he's been doing all of the things…
That a man should be doing for his children.

And less in want is what he expects…
Except for just a little bit of love.
And for it to be more in the way…
For them to just say, "Happy Father's Day."

Motherhood

It's a special time in life…
When a woman is to bear a child.
And if it's the first one to be…
It's a beautiful moment, when she conceives.

Because she'll experience motherhood…
And how it feels to care for a baby.
For it to come as naturally…
As she's expecting it to be.

Because a life is now entrusted to her…
For guidance to be with loving hands,
And with this precious gift she's been given…
It's to cherish for a lifetime.

For she'll learn about motherhood as she goes…
And how to manage a life with love.
Because she'll understand what she does…
By giving her baby, the love she's made of.

Mother And Daughter

From a mother to her daughter...
She passes on the gift of life,
One that she can give to another...
One day, in her lifetime.

Because she instills in her...
The instinctive values of being a mother.
With the relationship becoming...
A bonding of love and friendship.

And there will be times, to make amends...
When their directions in life don't blend,
Especially when a daughter grows up...
And her mother's influence comes to an end.

But a mother's love...
Will always be with her,
For her to always remember...
The love that was given.

Because it will be realized...
For the both of them to understand,
That the love they share together...
Will forever go on, between a mother and daughter.

Mother's Day

A day is set aside once a year...
For the celebration of motherhood,
In honor of her worth...
For all of her special work.

Because from nursing us through childhood...
We know of her importance.
And from preparations for our adulthood...
Our love is given to her in reverence.

Because she's the one that leaves the imprint...
With the stamp of her approval.
And she'll receive her gifts on Mother's Day...
With love and appreciation to come her way.

And for being humble...
She'll just say, she was just doing her job,
By just being a mother...
On just another beautiful day, for a loving mom.

"Call Momma!"

When you have good news…
"Call Momma."
And when you're lost and confused…
You better call her.

Because she's mainly the one that's concerned…
About your health and welfare.
And she's the one that cares to listen…
To the happiness and sadness you'll share.

And with her intuition about things in life…
She'll give words of wisdom to help you survive.
And you'll be in her prayers too…
When no one else is praying for you.

For you can count on her always…
To give love from the beautiful spirit of her karma.
For she feels what your soul needs before you do…
So for peace of mind in your heart, "Call Momma!"

"Momma, Said!"

Momma, said…
Be on your best behavior when you leave home,
Get a good education, along with humility…
And don't ever embarrass the family.

Momma, said…
Wear clean underwear wherever you go.
And don't make a fool of yourself…
If you come up short on the guest list.

Momma, said…
Always stand up for your rights.
And when you take a fall from grace…
Get back up and try to save face.

And Momma, said…
Be true to your word.
And let it be the bond…
That will let your integrity be heard.

And Momma, said…
There will be days like this and that.
And if they're filled with enough righteousness…
God will make sure, that you're always blessed.

Momma's Watching

If your mother could see you now…
You know what she would think.
And it would depend on the acclaim…
From a conscience of honor or shame.

Because she's instilled in us a sense…
To understand the spirit of right and wrong.
And it resonates through our souls…
When she's not around, and we're alone.

And it matters, to make all the difference…
If we can make her proud of us,
By winning in the game of life and honesty…
To say "Hi Mom, thank you for the victory."

Because we'll remember her instructions…
Of fairness, not warranting retributions,
While all the time trying to be on our best behavior…
Consciously knowing, that momma's watching.

"Happy Children's Day"

A day of all days, to be remembered…
A day to be celebrated.
One day out of the year…
To honor the children we love so dear.

Because they're a precious gift to the world…
Given to us on the day of their birth.
And it's with joy for every boy and girl…
To be rewarded with the gifts from our hearts.

For today is their day for offerings…
To be recognized for being the offspring,
The ones, who will pass on the genes…
In the continuing life of a family.

And with great appreciation, we'll give to them…
All of the wonderful things they've got coming,
First, in the ways of the love we'll share…
Then to just say, "Happy Children's Day."

Through The Eyes Of A Child

Another day passes by for a child…
As they look through the window of life.
To see what is to become to be…
From observations of the learning tree.

And they'll live within their imagination…
As reality grows in the minds of perception.
Trying to come to an understanding…
Of believing in what they can achieve.

For their visual conception begins…
At the moment they open their eyes.
And then, they begin to see with amazement…
All of the things in a life of wonderment.

And it all becomes of their innocence…
To be overwhelmed all the while.
For the truth to be seen in all of its essence…
As we should see it, through the eyes of a child.

The Children Are Listening

Just waiting to imitate us...
Kids, watching all of our moves.
Hearing and wondering...
Pondering on things to pursue.

The youngsters and their imagination...
Trying to make sense out of grownup conversation.
Figuring things out, right off the cuff...
With ears full of processing the information.

Hiding behind the couch...
Listening from around the corner.
Trying to blend in with the scenery...
Invisible to the gossip, and ready to spread the rumors.

And as real as Minnie and Mickey Mouse is to them...
Second star to the right with an adventurous Peter Pan,
Hanging on to every word about woman and man...
Taking a page out of the facts in the life of mankind.

And careful as it's said...
Quite is kept instead.
Because beyond the whispering...
The children are listening.

The Children Are Playing

They gather in the neighborhoods and on the playgrounds…
Waiting for the sun to go down.
They're so young in mind and at heart…
Not ready to go home right now.

But the day is ending…
And we would think, they had enough.
But the children are still playing…
Without a care in the world about us.

And as the understanding goes…
They'll try to play on.
Caught up in the moment…
With no second thoughts about the punishment.

For the children are out for the fun…
That comes with the territory of being young.
Playing all of the games as they do…
Before their youth grows old with the curfew.

"Child's Play"

We say no.
And they say yes.
We ask why?
And they say, why not!

Because as children play…
They re-invent the games,
That they learned from us…
To do the same.

And until they can discern…
The lessons from life to learn,
For them, it'll always be…
Just children doing what they see…

For they know no better…
But just the games people play,
Waiting to be taught the right way…
Before the fun and games are over.

Because when recess comes to an end…
With playtime at the end of a serious day,
Hopefully they'll grow up to understand…
That all it was then, was just "child's play."

"Can't Fool The Children"

Babies know who's genuine...
And can spot a fake a mile away.
Keeping them in mind all the time...
And every time they show their face.

Because the kids can feel it...
When it doesn't feel right.
And if it looks phony...
They'll know it at first sight.

For a child listens to the voice...
To realize when something's wrong.
And they know when someone is lying...
By the eyes, and the look on their face.

Because you have to be good at heart...
With sincerity coming from a good spirit within.
And it's not what's cute to say and do...
Because you can't fool the children.

A Poem For The Children

A celebration of a beautiful life to be…
Wishes upon a shining star,
Bearing gifts of all kinds…
Realizing the potential of a youthful mind.

And with a little imagination…
A cartoon and a favorite toy come to life,
All for a boy and girl…
To chase rainbows in a magical world.

And from birthday parties to Halloween…
Christmas time and spring break in between,
It's for the summertime to come in a flash…
Hotter than July, it passes by so fast.

And with the first day of school…
Comes the Golden Rule.
To do unto others…
As you would have them do unto you.

For happiness will come through yearning…
From kindergarten, to higher learning.
And as children, they'll grow up from the start…
With nursery rhymes, and poetry in their hearts.

When The Sun Rises

At first light, the day begins…
As it always never fails on its journey,
To start its climb at the dawning…
Spreading its warmth across the waters of life.

And upon the shores await the morning dew…
Collected with the mist from the rushing waves,
That splash upon the wind-swept faces…
Filtering in with the golden rays of sunlight.

For the beginning of a precious day continues…
Strolling over meadows and rolling hills,
While the sun is still rising to shine…
Going up mountainsides, and down into the valleys.

And the rest of the world, still in slumber…
Will have to wait their time on the rock,
To look over the horizon…
Anticipating the time, for when the sun rises.

Closer To One Family

Closer to being one nation of equality…
Is yet so far away to achieve.
And to be nearer to one world family…
Seems to be almost impossible to believe.

Yet, there is still hope…
Waiting on our doorsteps,
With a key in the only hand…
That can unlock the doors to peace.

Because there's no kicking it in…
We must pray for it to open.
Then we can feel welcomed of that…
As the words would say, on the doormat.

To come together as a family…
While being closer than we might think.
But knowing it's not enough to just say it…
Because talk is cheap these days.

For the actions we see from some of the clergy…
Are divided amongst themselves.
And the words we hear from the layman…
Are on par with a world going straight to hell.

And if we're waiting for our governments…
To answer the hard-pressed questions about our problems,
Many will be gone, before changing hands with time happens…
To be closer to one family, when God puts this system to an end.

Grandma

A baby is born of a new day...
Into the loving arms of a waiting mother.
And standing behind her in the wings...
Awaits the patience and love from a grandmother.

For she'll pick up the slack...
Through the years of this and that.
Being the one in the arrears...
To help dry up the little one's tears.

For her station in life...
Is to be a pillar of strength.
As strong as to be leaned upon...
Beyond the foundation of a guarantee.

Because with her hands...
She'll work the magic.
To weave into the hearts of the grandchildren...
Her personal strands of love and wisdom.

So when we need support...
To help shore things up with the children,
We know whom to call...
And it all comes back around, to Grandma.

Grandpa

A grandfather has his role to play...
In how he'll spoil the grandchildren.
But all the while, making sure...
To balance the act, before going too far.

Because it's all in the cards of wisdom...
For him to play the games of their hearts,
By bouncing babies on his knees...
And bringing a little joy and laughter to the scene.

For he'll earn his keep...
Through time well spent,
And by dancing to their tune...
While spending a little cash.

And he'll always be remembered...
For the status of being the patriarch of the family.
And with love to give, he'll just love to be called...
"Grandpa," That's all!

"Get It Done, Miss Jones!"

Deadlines come and go…
From business deals to washing clothes.
With no time to say no…
But to get it done, "Miss Jones."

Because mandates are set…
For work and play to be met,
With their priorities in place…
Scheduled for no delays.

And to keep all of the appointments…
Is for all that it takes to save the day,
While the movie is being made…
With a reoccurring role on instant replay.

And as the sun comes up…
Don't let it go down for nothing.
With no excuses, but for the results to come…
And to just, "Get it done, Miss Jones!"

"Get It Done, Mr. Jones!"

No matter how long it takes…
On the quest for conquest,
Never to put it to rest…
But to get it done, "Mr. Jones."

And with strong convictions in mind…
Feed the ambition of your potential.
Never to become disheartened…
Never to become disenchanted.

Because it's by the sure will of character…
And the force of your capability,
To anticipate each situation…
When you have to act on your ability.

For it to all come to completion…
Often with the forfeit of fun,
For when you have to get serious…
To just, "Get it done, Mr. Jones!"

"The Three Sisters"

There are one, two, three of them...
Three from two precious parents are they.
All from the same cloth...
Identical in the values they were taught.

And raised with loving care were they...
Aware of not to follow the Pied Piper.
And unlike the story of Cinderella...
All were qualified to wear the silver slipper.

Because each one carries their sleeping beauty...
To bear witness to their beautiful spirit.
And as their loveliness of character awakens,
It testifies to the attractiveness of their countenance.

For they've learned in life how to act...
And not to be upstaged by the sisters from nirvana.
But to leave their own legacies and legends...
As "The Three Sisters," from San Diego, California.

The Legacy Of LaVoyne

The life that she led...
Was in line with her belief in God,
Because it was filled with goodness...
And it always came forth in the form of kindness.

For she was truly of the kind...
To share her love with family and friends.
And she never did mind...
To lend a helping hand, from beginning to end.

And she was loved by all who knew her...
Because sharing and caring was what she was all about.
And without a doubt, she'll be remembered...
By all of what God's love will render.

For through his son Jesus Christ...
The way was paved for her to follow.
And she followed that path without wavering...
For all to know where she was going.

Because part of her spirit is here to show us...
And it's in all of us to know,
That God said, she's not gone...
For a love remains, in the life and legacy of LaVoyne.

"The Brothers Four"

The four from California...
In place of the good in each other,
And for all of the reasons in the world...
To befriend as many as they could.

For it was to each his own...
To learn from the other ones at home.
And as it is in the ways of brothers...
It was playtime, until it was time to be grown.

Then separate ways they went...
But not to forget the love,
For when life comes full circle...
They'll remember what it was all for.

And in the dominance for each one to control...
It's natural in the made-to-order male society,
To succeed, but not at the cost of what for...
Especially the love, from the "Brothers Four".

My Brother Richard

Blessed be the ones…
Who have a hand in the Lord's business,
Just as it is for all of the ones…
Who have it in their minds to finish.

And as did he…
My brother Richard,
He learned of God's words…
That continued to live in his heart.

And he brought them to song…
As we all knew he could sing.
And we knew he was testifying…
When he was caught up in the moment.

For it was always a Heavenly choir…
When he was in chorus with the Angels.
And it was always very special…
For all in harmony to witness.

And as it was for me…
I had the pleasure,
Of being raised as his twin…
Engaged in concert with him.

But his greatest act on Earth…
Was taking care of his family.
And with this love we can all attest…
To the fact that Jesus would say,
He was one of the best.

God bless you, my brother Richard.
You will be missed.

In God's Memory
(My Brother Fred)

We all pray we're in God's memory...
Having faith in that He'll remember us.
And on that last day and hour...
We'll hope that we've done enough.

And in our private resolve...
We'll know He understands,
How hard we've tried...
To live by His words.

And it is the belief that my brother Fred...
Came to a final conclusion,
To make his peace known...
With the God that would bring him home.

For he believed in the power...
That stood by hour after hour.
Keeping vigilance from the watchtower...
For deliverance into paradise.

God bless you, Fred
You will be missed.

Our Parents

Parents know when to get involved…
And when to stay away,
But while listening to what's being said…
They know better, not to look the other way.

Because they have a say so…
In what their children are doing.
Being aware of what they don't know…
And how and when, to say yes or no.

And with their tough love…
A child will know what it's all for.
Especially when it's time for knowing…
What's going on behind closed doors.

Because being suspicious is one of the ways…
Of showing their concern.
And with the discipline, they'll show the love.
That comes with affection in return.

And the children will respect it…
When they see the shining examples they expect,
From the parents, who are the role models…
They'll imitate, and want to follow.

"Heaven Knows Your Name"

Forgotten by mankind…
About as fast as you become old.
But remembered by God…
As your life unfolds.

And many will forget your name…
Just as soon as you say it.
And many will never know your quest…
Except if you become famous for it.

And by word of mouth…
Reputations are built upon.
And after the lights go dim…
Some legacies will never live on.

Because it's common to be forgotten…
But it's of your essence that remains.
For everything about you will be remembered…
Because Heaven knows your name.

"The Best!"

The best is yet to come…
As long as you make it so.
For what is done in practice…
Is made in the mindset of perfection.

Because it's positively paramount…
To be at your best in the endeavor.
For what is meant by second-best…
Is not good enough to pass the test.

For the standards are high…
On the list of not being denied.
And on goes the training…
Until you're satisfied.

Because sometimes the difficult things…
You can do right now.
But the impossible things…
Will have to take a little while.

And in time, even you'll be amazed…
At what they thought you couldn't do.
And it's with praise, not to be fazed…
Because that's just what the best do.

Never Surrender

Never give in to the evil...
That swarms like bees protecting the hive.
Because you'll be imprisoned with the sin...
Outside of trying to stay alive.

Never give in to the doubt...
Thinking it can't be done.
Because before you get started...
You won't know where you're coming from.

And never give in to losing...
Knowing you could have won.
Especially when practice makes perfect...
And perfect practice will get it done.

And never surrender to the life and times...
That don't register in the headlines.
Because every day they'll pay you a visit...
To remind you, that you're on the front lines.

"Be Honest With Yourself!"

Only you know how bad you can get…
And how good you want to be,
With the evidence to surmise…
That it's not guesswork, to be realized.

But it's to suppose that you know…
The difference between right and wrong,
And the good and the bad in things…
That belong to a measure of honesty.

Because the lie will fail in the arena…
As the truth prevails in the Colosseum.
For the gladiators will battle over your conscience…
With the clash of the Titans in your mind.

And in remembering what you already knew…
You'll know when to take it to the canvas.
And to fight for the home front advantage…
To feel good about getting up with yourself.

For you may forget the song and dance…
But you'll never forget how it made you feel,
With a melody that carried you along…
And words to sing, that couldn't be wrong.

Because what's right about it…
Is that it feels good to be justified,
Not to be fooled by anything else…
But at first, is to be honest with yourself.

You're Never Alone

God is always with you...
With spiritual guidance to give you.
So take care in that you have his support...
For he knows the condition of your heart.

Because you can rely on his words alone...
To give you comfort through the days and nights,
Being sure of his promises to keep...
To send the power in the spirit of relief.

For when you feel there's no way out...
Put on the breastplate of faith.
Because you'll need the protection and strength...
To help bring the darkness into the light.

Because you're never alone...
When you follow the 'Light of the World.'
And you'll always be out in a crowd...
When you follow the truth in God's words.

For when you're standing shoulder to shoulder...
With God, the Son and the Holy Spirit,
Just remember the company you're in, when you're lonely...
And you'll never be alone again.

Your Daily Bread

It's food for thought to live by…
A crust of bread as such to receive.
It's the nourishing words of God's spirit…
Giving you the peace of mind you'll need.

For as you go about your daily routine…
You'll have a full plate to deal with.
Because there's a hungry world out there…
And you'll be the main course, if you don't beware.

And with the right kind of sustenance…
Life becomes of the measurement,
To balance the scales of your lifestyle…
With righteousness to dine at the Lord's Table.

Because you'll need every morsel…
No matter how you slice up the day.
And before breakfast, and before you go to bed…
Don't forget to partake, of your daily bread.

A New Attitude

A new look...
New clothes and shoes,
A new hairdo with a smile...
And you've got a new attitude.

Because all of these things...
Will build your confidence,
To a level you can understand...
To be in, and of itself.

And with an attitude on the make...
Comes a new outlook.
Seeing you, for what you were...
And being, what you've become.

And with a new point of view
You'll have a new vision to follow.
And then after your transition...
You'll have a different disposition.

And with a new attitude...
You'll look at things differently,
Putting your mind into the frame...
Of a new portrait, of yours truly.

Find A Way

Whatever the task at hand...
It shouldn't matter at all.
For whatever the job demands...
It stands to reason, to answer the call.

And if it's a tall order to fill...
You know the drill,
Not to come up short...
When it counts the most.

For when you're in dire straits...
You have to explore every phase,
From all of what you're made of...
To discover a way through the maze.

Because day after day will come...
With your willpower on display.
And some way, somehow without delay...
Through the matrix, find a way.

The Fear Of Failure

Failing to try, is the fear…
Leaving you more than bewildered.
And if you never get past that act…
You'll always be too afraid to try.

Because fear is part of the unknown…
Shaking the will to go on.
And whenever failure is implied…
Failing is not far behind.

For when your confidence is shaken…
Your willpower will be tested.
And then here come the excuses…
And there goes your chances.

Because now you've set it up…
Preparing for yourself to fail,
And losing out on the opportunity…
To feel the thrill of victory, and to prevail.

And to continue on like this…
Would not be a wise investment.
For perseverance is the testament…
To fear not, the failure to resolve.

Failure Is Not An Option

Never let it cross your path…
To falter at any time.
Because it's all-consuming to the mind…
For problem-solving of any kind.

Because negative thoughts will breed regrets…
And after that, there's no turning back,
Unless a positive mind overcomes…
All the right reasons to get things done.

And not to waste any time worrying…
Or in dwelling on the fear of failing.
Because it's a lost cause to think…
To give it any thought at all.

Because failure is not an option…
Especially when there's a tax on falling behind.
For the cost of living is always on the line…
And winning is mandatory, all of the time.

Hardball

It's a game time situation...
With your life on the line.
It's a full count in the ninth inning...
And the home team is no longer winning.

So now it's time to bear down...
And to keep your eyes on the prize.
Because it means a win or a loss...
In the final game of life's playoffs.

And as many are counting on you to succeed...
It's not the time to slack.
For the pressure goes beyond Little League...
With Big Time decisions running a fast pace.

For we know what you've done in the past...
With all of your capabilities to date.
And when you step up to the plate...
We're expecting to hear the crack of the bat.

And until you come through...
Many eyes will be watching and waiting.
Because you're playing a life of hardball...
And it's "World Serious," so go down swinging.

A Reality Check

Stop! And take a look around...
At what's really going down.
And take a reality check...
To avoid the train wreck.

Because warning signs are everywhere...
And they're lit up like Christmas trees.
And if you still believe in Santa Clause...
Then you're living in the fantasyland of make-believe.

Because there are no gifts underneath the trees...
For just being the good boys and girls.
And we'll have nothing coming without faith...
But just another day of surviving in this world.

And if we're fortunate enough to get past the day...
We'll still have to deal with the night.
Because while we're asleep, our minds are on deck...
And when we awaken, it's a reality check.

"Do It For You!"

Do all the good you can for yourself…
Because you never know when you can't.
And do all of the righteous things in life…
For Heaven and people on earth to be a witness.

Because your reputation is at stake…
To build upon the make and model.
And your legacy is on the line…
To leave the tracks of your best footsteps behind.

For you to do what you love the most…
And along the way, get some respect for it.
Doing all that you can…
To make them want to remember you for it.

And do onto others…
As you would have them do unto you.
Do it for family and friends, do it for mankind…
Do it for the God of love, and "Do it for you!"

"The Table"

A feast fit for royalty...
Take a seat at the table.
A banquet good enough for nobility...
Gracing a meal for humanity.

And with food production at an all-time high...
It's more than enough to fight worldwide famine,
Minus the economics, distribution and the waste...
All to take their place, at the table.

Because communication is the factor...
Conversation is a must,
With problem-solving at best,
All involved in trust... at the table.

Breaking bread, sipping wine...
The "Last Supper."
Blessings for all to find peace of mind...
Invitations to come and dine, at "The Table."

"American Made"

From the very beginning of our thirteen colonies…
It was made-to-order, to make everything within it.
And as we grew in the spirit of resourcefulness…
We even made a way for our independence.

And from the homespun clothes we wore…
To the shoes on our feet,
We made everything we could think of…
To everything we dreamed about.

And with some good old-fashioned Yankee ingenuity…
We became the world's largest manufacturer.
And a path was beaten to our door…
To want more of what we had in store.

So then, we began to outsource the work…
For cheaper labor, for a lesser price to pay.
And now we're buying inferior products…
For a throw-away society to have its day.

And if we don't turn it around, we'll lose out…
For we've seemed to have lost our way.
Because it used to mean, from out of the past…
That if it was made in America, it was made to last!

The Therapy Of Poetry

Inside the inspiration of a world of words…
Outside awaits the reality.
And beyond the realm of imagination…
Universal challenges prey on our mentality.

And between the poetic reflections…
We'll walk the fine line.
With life's confusions on our minds…
Waiting for the hand of reasoning to be kind.

To write the verses of compassion…
In the common language of the human experience.
Reading into it for the treatment…
With an understanding of it, for the contentment.

And it begins with the spirit of knowing…
When to step out of the shadows into the light.
And it continues with a mindset to believe…
In the powers of healing, in the therapy of poetry.

Lifestyles

Of the rich and famous...
Minding their business.
Of the poor and hapless...
Humbled and hoping for assistance.

Of the bad and treacherous...
Doing what they do to be wrong.
Of the good and righteous...
Sowing seeds before God's throne.

Of the forlorn and lonely...
Looking for love to come.
Of the happy and contented...
Loving life as it becomes.

Of the alternative ways and means...
Judged not to throw the first stone.
Of the norm by nature's order of things...
Lifestyles in the glasshouse of home.

True Gold

True gold doesn't need refinement…
For from the fire it pours as pure.
To be of its own precious quality…
Revealing the properties of its worth.

And its measurements…
Are by the proportion of karats.
And compared to your status…
You're worth your weight in gold.

For the importance of it…
Is by the market.
With the price of it…
Going up every day.

Because true gold doesn't depreciate…
It comes from the earth to remain the same.
And in you, we can relate it to…
Everything that appreciates with value.

Of All Faiths

Believing in what we've been taught...
And what life has wrought,
Living beyond the sacred pages...
By the words of truth upon stages brought.

And in the many aspects of tradition...
It's inherent to be receptive,
To the cultural exchange...
From conception, to the end of the mission.

For ideologies are framed...
Around pictures painted in a spiritual world,
Of the patriarchs and matriarchs...
From the prophets, down to the Messiah.

And the way will be led through world religions...
Not leaving any souls to fate,
For Divine providence to create...
The same righteous people, of all faiths.

"We're Counting On You"

Your family is relying on you…
Always with interest in what you do,
Just as good friends will confide in you…
For the strength in you, to see things through.

Because there's no holding back the winds…
That will blow in and out of your favor.
And there's no stopping the sunrises and sunsets…
That will rise and fall on your behalf.

And as some things become hard to control…
Most things in life can be managed.
And with Jehovah, God the Father by your side…
All is well, to warrant the advantage.

Because it all adds to your worth…
That has multiplied since your birth,
To take one step for Jesus Christ…
And two steps for righteousness and success.

For you're only as good as you want to be…
And a good-natured spirit will take you there.
And it's paramount that you follow through…
Because, we're counting on you.

"Finish It!"

Starting out anew...
Not forgetting the past.
Especially all of the uncompleted things...
That time didn't bring to task.

Because life within itself...
Is forever filled with unfinished business,
While living on the side of procrastination...
Will store more dreams in the attic.

For sometimes it takes extra steps...
To turn the corner on success.
And it always takes determination...
To bring anything to fruition.

Because the fruit will fall from the tree...
But not too far, to just let it be.
For the table is set to partake of it...
With a full plate, waiting for you to "finish it!"

The American Dream

America's dreams are fading…
Like a sunset on the west coast.
And the nightmares are awash…
With a sunrise to witness the ghost.

For we've mortgaged our future rites-of-passage…
To live way beyond our means.
And we've cashed-in on our tomorrows…
To leave a house full of debt for our children.

And now, a day of reckoning has arrived…
Due to the "Great American Experiment."
And it's dead on arrival, with apple pie…
Waiting for a revival from the experience.

Because now it's time to brace for impact…
And take-stock in standing up.
Never to quit and never to give up…
For still alive are all of the things…
That make up, the American Dream.

Dreams Into Reality

Earthly changes to come...
A paradise to hope for.
Spiritual transformations to come...
A heavenly revelation to live for.

With faith, to awaken in the flesh...
Then, a revealing of the spirit.
With feelings of what we've wished for...
To be in the peaceful realm we've prayed for.

And the reasons are to dream...
Of waterfalls flowing into streams,
With a countryside flourishing in spring...
As blessings of sunshine nourishes our well-being.

And in good faith with the things we've imagined...
Of living in the serenity of love and harmony,
While believing we're not out of reach of eternity...
We'll turn our dreams into realities.

Blessed

The sun comes up on another day…
Rising with the beauty of life.
And as we walk this earth with all of its gifts…
We're blessed to see the light.

For it becomes of the living…
To know what they've been given.
And it's for everyone to realize the value…
Of all the provisions coming from Heaven.

And blessed be the one…
Who follows the path of righteousness.
And blessed be it to all…
Who continue to call on the Lord.

For the blessings will be poured out…
To drink of the pure goodness within.
And when all is partaken of and assessed…
You'll know in your heart, that you've been blessed.

The Learning Process

From conception, we begin the miracle of life...
And while in the womb, we experience survival.
And after birth, it becomes of the awareness...
That living on "Mother Earth" is a learning process.

Because we learn of the nourishment we need...
From mother's milk, to what the land provides.
And then we'll begin to feel the spirit...
From all of what God has put in it.

And from our mind, body and soul...
We'll direct our thoughts to be selective.
Educating ourselves to what we think is best...
To live, off of what's in our best interest.

For we'll learn of the good and bad things...
To know what they mean to become.
And we'll understand right and wrong...
Enough to decide which one belongs.

And in our makeup of the cosmos...
We'll explore the mysteries of the universe,
Enough to discover, that it's all for us...
And that it's all in part, of the learning process.

"Trust In Me"

When things have gone awry in your life...
And you've been losing ground with the truth,
To where the foundation of your temple is crumbling...
God says, "Put your trust in me."

When all hope is slipping away...
And your faith is fading fast,
While each day looks like it might be the last...
God says, "Put your trust in me."

And when you meet your character on the street...
And you don't recognize your reputation,
And lost in the shuffle is your integrity...
God says, "Put your trust in me."

And when your countenance is at a loss in the race...
Because your footsteps have betrayed you,
And your spirituality has to face the reality...
God says, "Put some trust in yourself."
"Trust me!"

The River Of Life

Tributaries full of life...
Streams flowing with a zest for living.
Rippling springs and babbling brooks in rhythm...
Rivers running with the current of time.

And at the source of each odyssey...
Are all of the helping hands.
And it's for all hands on deck to be ready...
As we embark, for the high-water mark.

Because we'll ride the rapids...
Hanging on for dear-life.
And we'll sail along on the calm waters...
With the winds of time at our backs.

And with a thirst for living...
We'll drink from the well of our delights,
To guide the ship through troubled waters...
As we travel up and down, on the river of life.

The Trees Of Life

The tree of life...
Growing from out of the Garden of Eden.
Bearing fruit that was meant for us...
A must for our survival.

For the provisions are there...
To share in the care of our welfare.
From the building of houses, to nutrition...
And to the direct correlation with the air we breathe.

And from the birds and the bees...
To the flowers and the trees,
We live for procreation...
For the continuation of the human family.

Because from the burning bush...
We learned of God's plan,
For the direction of man...
To occupy the land flowing with milk and honey.

And it's all for us to enjoy the gifts...
That the trees of life provide.
Because without them, we're dead in the water...
And we'll never, ever survive.

"The Poet Says"

The poet says:
"Life is short,
The days are long…
Always to long for more."

The poet says:
"Dying comes easy,
Living is hard…
In times of trying, there's no denying."

The poet says:
"Sleep is precious,
Waking up is glorious…
Work and play are underrated."

And the poet says:
"Love is full of potential,
Time is of the essence…
Embrace the day," the poet says.

Behind Every Good Man

Born from woman…
He makes his stand.
With dreams of prosperity…
He makes his plans.

And while on his run to the top…
He's stopped by many roadblocks.
But then, she reports to work…
To shore him up, with her support.

Because when things go awry…
She's right there by his side.
Looking in the face of his distress…
To give him the confidence he'll need to address.

For in being his companion…
She'll be the one counting on him, and demanding.
For when the storm winds are blowing…
He'll still be standing.

Because she has a stake in his progress…
Being his natural partner in the process.
And as his complement, there she stands…
Along with the success that awaits, behind every good man.

For The Rest Of His Life

Men, get ready to pay up...
For playing the dating game.
Men, get ready to pay more...
For the hard work in the institution of marriage.

Because all is well, when at first they meet...
Dinner, dancing, taking her to the movies.
And all is to be continued, when at last they met...
Picking up the tab, for everything she gets.

For once he starts going down that road...
It's never ending for him.
Because he'll be paying through the nose...
And that's just how it goes.

Because here comes her birthday...
A day he should never forget.
And then, comes a St. Valentine's Day gift...
And the buying of an Easter Sunday outfit.

But in relief, he may get a pass on Halloween...
And he'll surely get a meal on Thanksgiving Day.
But after a night of sleep, he'll wakeup to hear...
Money is needed for a shopping spree on Black Friday.

And before Holy Matrimony...
He'll spring for the engagement, and the wedding ring.
And after the Honeymoon...
He'll be paying for everything.

And after the love tokens...
And after the gifts of appreciation,
And if there are children in the nest, and the like...
He'll be paying for the rest of his life.

Live, To Be Remembered

Leading a good life…
Will attest to the goodness of your character.
Leading a righteous life…
Will be a testament to the spirit of your soul.

For as you grow to get old…
Everyone you know, will know the path you've taken.
And everyone they've known will be told…
About the road you've traveled.

And every place your heart has touched…
Your tracks will tell the story,
Hopefully speaking, with all of the accolades…
That will testify about the legacy of your glory.

For when they see the light from within…
They'll see the starlight shining beyond,
With all of the good things you've done…
For you to remember…to live, to be remembered.

Remembering Them

It's like a 5-Star movie still in the running...
Starring some of the special people we've known:
The family members, the friends...the loved ones...
All of the ones that have gone on to glory.

Never to forget their essence...
As we'll forever recall the reruns of their acts.
Remembering them, for what they still mean...
Praying to believe, that we'll see them again.

And as reminiscing comes to mind...
The precious memories keep coming to reside,
With the countenance of peace by our side...
As their angelic faces appear to come alive.

Because it seems like it was just yesterday...
When last night, they were here.
And we were together in the sunlight of life...
Enjoying beautiful sunrises and sunsets.

For as we keep their memories alive...
Their spirits will never die.
And until it's God's will for our time to end...
We'll live on, to always be, remembering them.

The Shining Examples

Twinkle, twinkle, all of those stars...
It's of wonder, how they got that far.
For in the life of growing up...
They are the ones, we look up to from afar.

And it should be, your father or mother,
Your sister or your brother.
Or your grandfather or grandmother,
Or all of the stellar ones from past and present.

And whomever it is to be imitated...
Let it be of the ones with integrity.
Smart enough to fill your heart...
With all of the good things to impart.

For of the intellectuals...
Or just on the average,
They manage someway, somehow...
To go to the head of the class.

And to shine as the brightest star...
Just like the righteous and the prosperous do.
To be one of the shining examples...
For others to follow suit, right behind you.

Inspiration

The rising sun...
Coming up in all of its splendor.
A day unfolds...
Untold are the many things to render.

A snowflake falls...
None are the same.
The stars shine on a clear night...
Imagination reigns.

A pure expression of spiritual faith...
Visits to the heart and soul of love.
Reaching for the stars in your eyes...
Searching for answers from the Heavens above.

Full of a life to live...
Much in the way of exploration.
With each discovery, a new sensation...
Again it comes, full of inspiration.

Stay Focused

A mind going adrift sometimes…
Wandering everywhere.
Mind over matter if you don't mind…
Wondering if you care.

Not to be held hostage…
By not paying attention.
When to be committed…
To cash-in on some discipline.

Sipping the cup of coffee if you must…
Staying alert through the coldest of nights.
Drinking ice water in the heat of days…
Wiping the sweat off your brow as you might.

And with eyes that light up for knowledge…
From whatever comes under the microscope.
It's for you to study the big picture as it unfolds…
And beyond being adrift, stay focused.

Confidence

Bring your confidence with you...
When you walk through the doors of opportunity.
And take it on the road...
Wherever your travels in life unfold.

Because you'll need it...
When you make your run for the gold.
And you have to feel it in your heart and soul...
Then you have to believe it.

For with self-assurance at the forefront...
Losing takes a backseat to winning.
And every time you take a loss...
It's not the end, but the beginning.

Because when you bring your best every day...
There's no way you can deny the essence.
For through adversity, it builds character...
To need nothing else, but your confidence.

Some Kind Of Poet

Many will find the words to express...
In some kind of form or fashion,
And more than likely with a mindset...
As common to the language of the human experience.

Because it comes from the feelings of expression...
For an imagination to take hold,
Of what is to behold...
From the past, present, and the future to be told.

And it will be for the insight...
To write the poetry to recite,
That fills in the silence of nights...
With the imagery of sounds in light.

And with the rhyme and reason for things...
Reflections of life become the writings of time,
And of the meaning in prose to note...
With words from the heart, from some kind of poet.

Words And Music

Music and words...
Set the stage for the dance,
And for the romance with a life...
That lives to realize its importance.

For in the words of a song...
We'll listen to identify with it.
And we'll hear enough to love the sensation...
With the poetic reflections in all its creation.

And with a melody to soothe our nature...
We'll feel the rhythm in the vibrations,
Taking our spirit on a magical journey...
With the instruments of musical expressions.

For in the consciousness of our receptiveness...
We'll choose the songs from sadness to bliss,
All for the personal reasons in our hearts...
Composed from the soul, of words and music

Saving The Best For Last

Be it just enough for now…
For then awaits the time to win it,
Being in the thick of the contest…
For how and when to end it.

Because you'll set the pace…
For the race to be had.
Sizing up the desire…
When it goes down to the wire.

For when it's expected of you…
You have to prove it.
Laying it all on the line…
When you're running out of time.

Because success awaits the endeavor…
For as long as you can attest,
To calling on all that you have left…
Saving the best for last.

A Prayer And A Promise

We go through life...
On a hope and a prayer.
Thanking the Lord every day...
For our being here.

To live for the promises...
That our prayers will be answered.
Knowing that a promise was made...
To ask, and we shall receive.

For we'll make it known of our desires...
In our prayers from the heart.
And we'll live off the words of wisdom...
To believe in due time, that we'll get the blessings.

Because God knows of the things we need...
And we know it will not be compromised.
For it comes with a love and the compassion...
From a prayer and a promise.

From Heaven To Earth

There's a place called Heaven…
And there's a planet named Earth,
Where mankind lives…
To love them both.

For what we know about Heaven…
We've learned through God's words.
And it dwells within us from birth…
To learn all we can about this earth.

Because we're still gaining knowledge…
About the ground we walk on.
And we're still acquiring wisdom…
From God's spiritual kingdom.

To believe in what we can't see…
And what we can feel of its worth,
For as it is in Heaven…
So it will be on Earth.

And from Earth to Heaven…
We'll communicate through prayers from the heart.
And with our faith, we'll have hope…
In the love that comes, from Heaven to Earth.

For As Long As You Live

As long as life goes on...
There's a promise made to everyone.
And if you make amends...
You'll receive all that you need in the end.

Because the God of all things...
Has balanced the scales to be in your favor.
And if you follow His path...
You will not fail in the endeavor.

For you'll acquire all of the benefits...
From a love that comes from within,
For as long as you believe...
For as long as you have faith in Him.

Because you'll reap from a harvest of love...
All you'll need, with enough to give.
To sustain you through life...
For as long as you live.

God Is Good

God is a good God...
He's a wonderful counselor to all.
And He's a compassionate savior...
With a strong hand for righteousness.

Because sometimes His powerful will...
Is too much for us to understand His ways.
For He did say, He was a jealous God...
And with vengeance, He would repay.

And if we believe in the punishment...
Of Hell's fire from down below,
For a short season on earth...
This cannot be good for mankind's worth.

Because God's spirit is of goodness...
He's a loving father to His children.
And whenever our time comes for mercy...
We'll get what we've got coming.

Because when we stop to realize His magnificence...
We'll see the beauty of His creation's plans,
Enough to have faith with full assurance...
In the goodness of God's promises, for us in this land.

Expect To Win

Don't come in thinking you might lose...
Just because the competition is stiff.
And don't play it down before it's over...
But instead, expect to be victorious.

Because your confidence will be a major factor...
To home-in on the zone.
Erasing all the doubt in the house...
To put your mind in the winning mode.

Then, to be sure of yourself...
Expecting to serve notice.
Posting it in your heart...
To recollect it, right from the start.

For when you come up against opposition...
Know the situation you're in.
And from the beginning until the end...
Expect to win.

"Rise And Shine"

A restful night…
From a sleep, full of dreams.
Sheets and bedspreads to shed…
Opened eyes, looking ahead.

Wiping off the comfort of warmth…
Stretching with the effort of a sunrise,
Reaching inside the sanctuary of a bedroom…
Where the light of enlightenment shines with insight.

Getting up with the sun's rays of gold…
Being up for a day to behold.
Washing the sleep off a fresh face…
Anticipating the race for progress.

And as part of the playbook becomes business…
In the twilight hour of pleasure, it comes with time,
To lay it down, before the night…
Blessed it be again, to rise and shine.

The Great American Stage

American classics have graced this stage...
Along with an array of other plays.
And as history was made in the New World...
So were the events to be staged.

And up from the ground it was built upon...
The wooden structures became,
As they were a place for entertainment...
Giving a platform for engagements.

And the ideas flowed as water...
Streaming through minds of creativity,
Bringing the arts to the theatre...
From where the heart of imagination begins.

For still is the night...
But just as bright as the day.
As the stage never sleeps...
It's awake with the dawn and the sunset.

To always be a part of the land...
Never to stop going its way.
Down that road we go again...
On the Great American Stage.

When We Meet Again

The night called them before the throne…
And then they were gone, to stand alone.
Awaiting the light of God's love to restore them…
As each one is chosen to go back home.

And the day resurrected the memories…
All the ones that were the best of them.
Because the happiness survived the sorrow…
As we prayed for tomorrow, to see them again.

For we'll meet in the Garden of hope…
Where there's enough faith to go around paradise.
And we'll grow with the resources from Heaven…
To blossom in the peace of tranquility.

And we'll drink of the water from the Holy Spirit…
And dine off the words of wisdom.
Giving praise to the Father and the Son…
For the love in our lives, when we meet again.

Forever Never Ends

Eternity awaits all of the believers...
Believing in what they think forever means.
And as time has its place in our observations...
We'll hold fast with faith, in trying to solve the equation.

For the timelessness can't be measured...
But to live forever is with hope to treasure.
Because with all of our calculations...
Our time on this planet outdates our estimations.

And as we're still adding up our time on earth...
We'll forever wonder about our time in the Garden,
And the sowing we've been doing ever since...
With the reaping we've been living with to accept.

And by all accounts on our imagination...
Our destination with time goes far beyond speculation,
Transcendent with the reality...
Of the spirit in life that lives forever.

Because first and foremost on our minds...
Is the mystery of time to comprehend,
As the beginning of time is to understand...
That time is forever, and forever never ends.

Peace In The Valley

There will be peace in the valley...
When all is said and done.
And it will come with satisfaction...
To be worth it to everyone.

And to all of the ones holding up...
Under the pressures of this world,
There's a reward for their faith...
Waiting beyond the Pearly Gates.

And in the valley...
They'll find all of the others,
That have earned their way by grace...
To live in this wonderful place.

Because there will be love...
There will be happiness,
And there will be peace...
In the valley of righteousness.

Young, Then Old

A young child's world without a care...
Ageless to even care to wonder.
Expecting to experience the fanfare...
Growing older, less the time to ponder.

The youth on the run at dawn...
No thoughts of a sunset after the fun.
The truth nipping at their heels...
Clocking time, with reality on track twenty-nine.

And from adolescence, to being a teenager...
Both have a short season to operate.
While the young adults live to reason with time...
Resigned to measure their future date with fate.

For when we were younger...
We couldn't wait to get older.
Young at first, to enjoy it...
Then old, before we know it.

When The Sun Sets

One thing we'll always remember...
Is when the end of the day comes.
With the work of it being over...
We'll wait on the setting sun...

And we'll witness how it slowly changes...
Into the colors of a breathtaking display,
Along with a relaxation it brings...
Settling the day, for the time to play.

Because the sun has done its job again...
And now it must surrender its light.
But not until it kisses the sky...
With a beauty it delivers before the night.

For in the twilight hour we'll see...
Shadows determining the time of day.
And they'll all fade away with the silhouettes...
To disappear, when the sun sets.